SEE THROUGH THE JUNGLE

By Millicent Selsam

Pictures by Winifred Lubell

HARPER & BROTHERS, PUBLISHERS, NEW YORK

SEE THROUGH THE JUNGLE

THE JUNGLE! Just the name is exciting. It makes us think of orchids and snakes, monkeys and twining vines. It is a forest, but it is not like any of the forests we know.

The jungles are the tropical tall green forests that cover the lands close to the earth's equator. Their scientific name is "rain forest." Almost ninety inches of rain falls on this forest belt every year—about three times more than the amount that falls on the average northern forest. As a result of the rain, and the nearness to the equator, there is a steaming hot climate that does

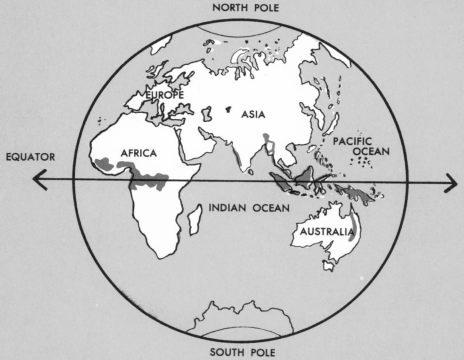

EASTERN HEMISPHERE

not change with the seasons. In fact, there is more difference in temperature between day and night than there is from one season to another. The trees stay green the year round. As old leaves fall, new leaves grow. Some trees are in blossom while ripe fruits are hanging on trees next to them.

There are great rain forests near the equator in Africa, on the Indonesian islands in the Pacific Ocean, and in Central and South America. The largest of these is in tropic America. Let's go there to see through the jungle, and explore it from bottom to top.

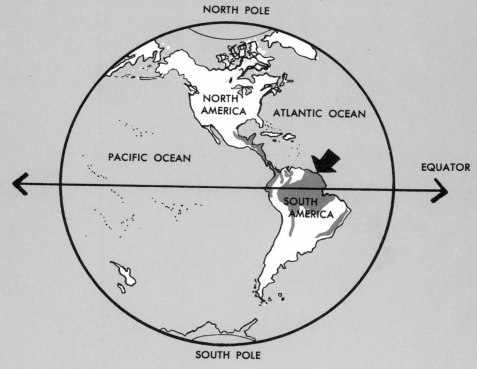

WESTERN HEMISPHERE

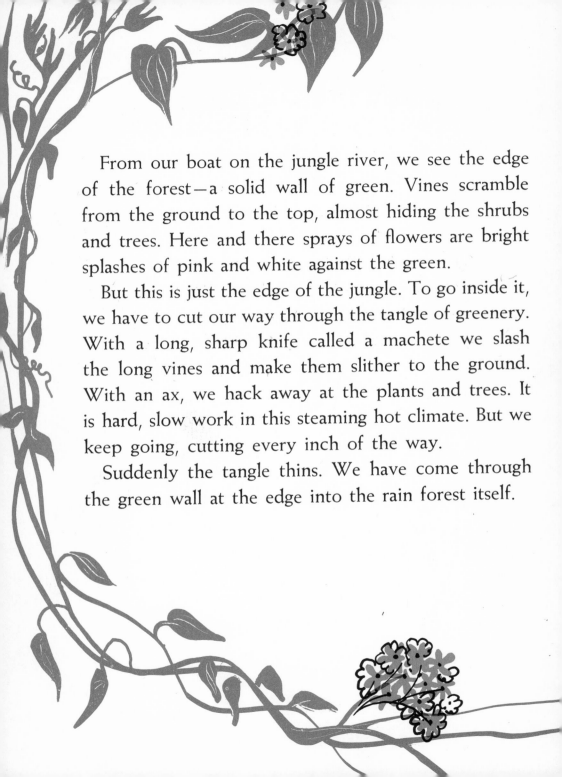

From our boat on the jungle river, we see the edge of the forest—a solid wall of green. Vines scramble from the ground to the top, almost hiding the shrubs and trees. Here and there sprays of flowers are bright splashes of pink and white against the green.

But this is just the edge of the jungle. To go inside it, we have to cut our way through the tangle of greenery. With a long, sharp knife called a machete we slash the long vines and make them slither to the ground. With an ax, we hack away at the plants and trees. It is hard, slow work in this steaming hot climate. But we keep going, cutting every inch of the way.

Suddenly the tangle thins. We have come through the green wall at the edge into the rain forest itself.

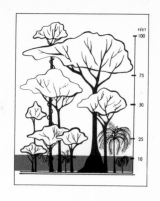

We are in a dim green world. Layer upon layer of leaves screen us from the burning hot sun. We can barely see the sky. Only here and there shafts of sunlight cut through the gloom. Vines, or lianas, are everywhere. Some are thin as strings, others thick as cables. Some are straight, some hang in loops, and some are twined around tree trunks. All are climbing to the upper stories of the forest where there is more light. There they pass from tree to tree and bind the treetops together. What a paradise for swinging! The thicker lianas are strong and can easily hold your weight.

Some of the vines have big, dark, shiny leaves. One or two of them look familiar to us. How can that be? We've never been to the jungle before. But some of the vines that grow wild here are popular house plants in the north. There is Monstera, called the Swiss cheese plant because of the natural holes in its deeply cut leaves. Climbing another tree is Philodendron.

Everywhere we look we see a different kind of tree. In a northern forest there are lots and lots of only a few kinds of trees—pines or oaks or maples. Here you would have to search to find two of the same kind of tree.

The trees look different from our northern trees, too. Look at the one that flares out at the bottom into a base or buttress that is almost as wide as a room. But most of the trees are tall and straight. We look up, up, and see hardly a branch till they reach the height of a six-story building. They, like the lianas, seem to be shooting straight up toward the light at the top of the forest.

There are smaller trees that seem to end where the giants begin to branch. Then there are still smaller trees that are only half as tall. How many layers of tree life there are in the tropical forest! It's like having three of our northern forests piled one on top of the other. Life is different in each of these forest layers. Let's see first what lives on the jungle floor.

100 FEET

90

80

70

60

50

40

30

20

10

The diagram will show you the level of the jungle we are exploring.

It is best to follow a trail in the jungle. Some parts of the jungle are easy to walk through, but you can lose your way too easily in these endless stretches of green wilderness.

From our trail we notice the ground plants. There are huge ferns, and palms with giant leaves springing right out of the ground. Many of the plants have large, soft, thin leaves splashed with white or gold or crimson. Here is the real home of some of our most beautiful ornamental house plants. You can probably recognize Caladium, with its leaves shaped like elephant ears, and the white-striped Dracaena.

As long as we walk along the trail making a great deal of noise we will not see many wild animals. If the animals see or hear or smell us first, they will either slip away or sit motionless. We have to be motionless ourselves, and melt into the background, to see the hidden life of the rain forest.

The time of day is important, too. Some of the jungle animals move about during the day, but many spend the day sleeping and come out only at night. To see both day and night animals we would have to pick a time at dusk, just before evening.

A strange-looking animal is waddling toward us on the trail. It has a nose like a nozzle, a tail like a huge brush, and legs that look like shaggy cowboy pants. This is the giant anteater. When it finds an ant nest, its powerful claws dig into it. Then it puts its nozzle nose down, and its long, thin, sticky tongue lashes out and collects the scurrying ants.

What a place for an anteater! In the tropical rain forest there are more ants than any other living thing. Large and small, brown, red, or black, they swarm everywhere.

Right near us a parade of leaves seems to be on the march! When we look closely, we see that it is really a procession of great red parasol ants. Each carries a piece of green leaf above its head like a parasol. They have cut these bits of leaf from the plants and are now taking them to their nest. There the ants will chew the leaves into a pulp which they lay down as a kind of soil. In this ant-made soil a special kind of mushroom grows. When the mushroom produces white juicy knobs, the ants feast. This is the only food they eat, and it grows only in the nest of the parasol ants.

Other columns of ants are moving in the forest. Usually a twittering of little ant birds tells us where the army ants are marching. In front of their columns is a mad scramble of crickets, spiders, roaches, beetles, and centipedes. They are all trying to get out of reach of the jaws of these insect-eating ants. The birds keep just ahead of the column and snap up what insects they can.

Another strange-looking animal is coming along now. This giant armadillo is covered with a skin of bony plates like a coat of armor. Like the anteater, it has a big claw on its front feet with which it can rip apart the nests of ants or termites. It, too, has a long tongue with which it laps up the insects.

If we get tired of standing still, we can try walking softly along the trail. It is surprising that we see so few flowers. Where are the tropical orchids we have heard so much about? We don't see a single one. Once in a while we notice the scarlet flower of the passion vine glowing in a small pool of sunshine. But there are few flowers growing in the dim light of the jungle floor. Their home is in the jungle roof high overhead where there is plenty of bright sunshine. Look down at your feet. The trail here is covered with bright flower petals and fruits that have dropped down from above.

One of the petals seems to be fluttering around. But there is no whisper of a wind down here. Look close. What we took for a petal is a butterfly with wings as clear as glass except for one brilliant spot of color.

As we walk, we stir up other butterflies and moths that were hovering over the leaves on the trail.

We must have been walking softly indeed. Near the wide base of that tree is a huge animal. The tapir has small ears, piglike eyes, and a snout like the beginning of an elephant's trunk. It is browsing on the leaves of the forest. Even though it is big, it is timid. We make a little noise, and it crashes away madly.

The tapir is frightened most of all of *el tigre*. This is the name South American people have given to the jaguar. The jaguar is a cousin to the tiger that prowls the jungles of Indonesia. It is a great yellow cat spotted with black. It can slip noiselessly along the jungle floor, or it can leap into the trees and walk along the branches. From them it can hurl itself through the air and pounce on its prey. One of its favorite dinners is the tapir. It also feasts on another common jungle animal—the peccary or wild pig of the forest.

Some peccaries must be near by right now. Their strong smell has just reached us. And suddenly we hear the clicking of their long, sharp tusks. Peccaries travel in herds from a few to several hundred strong. We know they won't purposely attack us. But all the same we take to the nearest tree. We would rather not be in the way.

The jungle does not drip with poisonous snakes. Most of the time we would see no sign of them. But it is just as well not to meet up with the deadly bushmaster, or the poisonous fer-de-lance.

We watch the trail carefully, for the bushmaster is hard to see when it is lying on the ground. Its mottled colors look like a bit of the jungle floor. The bushmaster is about seven feet long, and is the largest poisonous snake of the American tropics.

The fer-de-lance is hard to see, too. Its pattern and color also blend with the jungle floor. Its head, shaped like the point of a spear, gives it its name. Fer-de-lance is French for iron of a spear.

Our jungle trail has led us to a clearing. In this open space some giant trees have fallen, letting the sunlight through.

We are suddenly dazzled. Tropical plants that cannot grow in the dim gloom of the deep rain forest fill every inch here. It is as hard to get through here as it is at the edge of the jungle. Swarms of insects are buzzing and whirring. Beetles shimmer with gold, emerald, and ruby. There are clouds of bright butterflies. Some are velvety black swallowtails with crimson spots and little "tails" on their hind wings. Some are 88's—small bright butterflies with this number clearly showing on the underside of their hind wings, like the numbers on airplane wings.

The vines from the surrounding forest spill into the clearing. In this brilliant sunshine they burst into blossom. Hummingbirds sparkle in the light as they hover at these blossoms and suck their nectar.

The clearing is bright, buzzing, and full of colors.

Suddenly there is a rumble from the sky. A cloud passes over the sun, and in a few minutes we are in a terrific downpour. It feels more like standing under a waterfall than standing in the kind of rain we know in the north. Quickly we snap off some giant leaves, run back into the forest, and wait under our leaf umbrellas until the rain is over. It stops just as suddenly as it started. Once again shafts of sunlight enter the deep forest and the dripping wet leaves glitter.

All the time we are in the rain forest we hear rustling in the trees above us. What lives up there?

People who have gone to the rain forests on scientific expeditions have tried to find out by climbing the trees. But jungle trees are not easy to climb because most of them are so tall and straight and branchless. Some scientists have hammered giant spikes into the wood and climbed to platforms built at different levels in the trees. Even this is hard to do. Most of the trees here have such hard wood that they ring like metal to the blows of an ax. Only a few trees here are soft enough for spike ladders.

Some scientists have hauled rope ladders up to different heights in the trees. In other trees they have rigged up a rope and pulley and then hauled up a chair to the level they wanted. Here they could sit and watch the life in the trees. In both cases they needed the help of the native Indians. The Indians are skilled climbers. They wear spiked boots and use loops of rope passed around their bodies and the tree trunks. In this way they can get to the tops of even tall, straight trees. They carry rope lines that they pass over a branch high in the treetops. Then they haul up the ladders or swinging chairs.

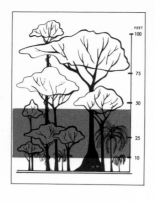

Let's try a spike ladder first. We clamber up to a platform about twenty-five feet above the ground. This brings us to the tops of the lowest trees.

Just below us is the top of a tree fern—a giant fern that spreads out like a huge green umbrella on top of a slender trunk. Long ago, way before the days of the dinosaurs, there were whole forests of tree ferns all over the world. Now these leftovers of a past age are found only in the tropics.

Next to the tree fern is a very strange tree—a cocoa tree. It grows wild here, but it is also cultivated on plantations to produce the cocoa we use. Its flowers seem to pop right out of the trunk and main branches. Only in the tropics do flower buds burst through the bark of trees in this way. When these flowers change to fruit, the tree will look even stranger, because the fruits are big and hang down like huge, rough lemons.

A curassow—a jungle turkey whose black feathers have a purple gloss—is perching in the cocoa tree.

Everything is so green here that we are delighted to see a party of Heliconia butterflies sailing below us, with bright spots of color on their black wings.

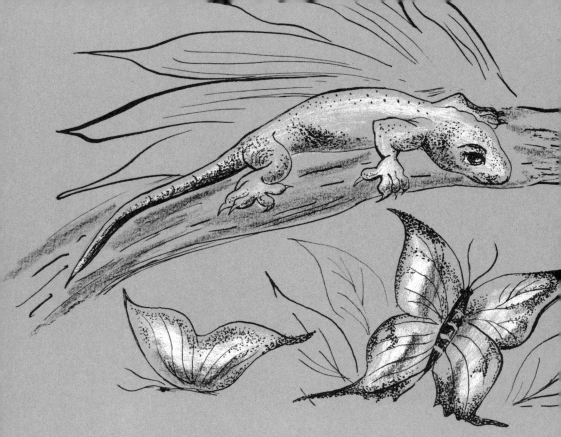

As we sit on our platform (when the ants let us), our eyes begin to pick out the smaller shapes of living things that are hard to see, even though they are quite near us.

A gecko lizard is close by, but its green color hid it from our eyes. The gecko is a lizard that can climb trees with the sticky pads on its toes. Near it is a leaf butterfly. Its folded wings look exactly like leaves, even to the marks and veins. If it hadn't moved in a peculiar way, we wouldn't have seen it at all. We hardly notice a twig on the branch next to us until it walks away! It wasn't a twig at all, but a giant walking stick.

These are only a few of the creatures of the rain forest that look like the place where they live. We need the keenest of eyes to find them. So do their enemies. The green color of the gecko, the leaf markings of the leaf butterfly, the twig shape of the walking stick, all *protect* them from the hungry creatures who are always hunting them. In every part of the rain forest we will find insects and other small animals that seem to melt into their background. This kind of "looking like the place where they live" is called *protective resemblance*.

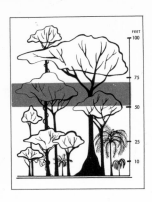

Now let's try a rope ladder to climb up to the middle level of the jungle. In this steaming hot land, climbing a ladder is hard work. The perspiration pours off our bodies and soaks into our clothes. When we reach our platform about fifty feet above the jungle floor, we are ready to rest.

We look quietly around. What a strange and lovely sight! Gardens are hanging in midair! Plants are growing in every nook and cranny and crack in the trees. We looked in vain for orchids below—they are here, perched in the trees. Near us is a spray of a lovely pink orchid. Each flower looks like a butterfly frozen in flight. Only a few of the orchids here are like the large gaudy types we see in flower stores. Most of them are small and delicate. Next to the pink orchid is a plant with a brilliant red flower in the center of a circle of leaves. The leaves look like those at the top of a pineapple.

The orchids, the pineapple-like plants called bromeliads, and the other plants we see up here on the trees are called *air plants* or *epiphytes*. They do not take their food from the trees on which they grow. They simply use the trees as perches. Then how do they get the water and minerals they need to live?

The roots of orchids form a woven mass like a sort of self-made flowerpot. In this tangled mat of roots, water and pieces of leaves and blossoms collect. As this plant material decays, it becomes a sort of soil that contains the minerals the air plants need.

The overlapping leaves of the bromeliads form a basin which catches and holds water and plant material. On the bottom of the leaves that line this "tank," there are tiny hairs that take in the water and minerals.

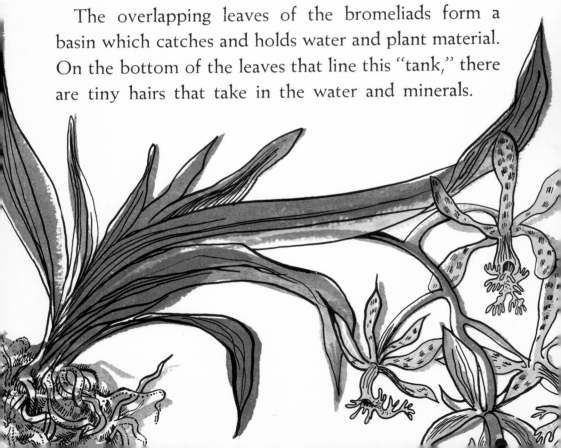

We tear a leaf off one of the bromeliads. Water splashes all over us. We have disturbed a whole little animal world that lived inside the pool of water held by the clasping leaves. Tiny froglets, beetles, ants, millipedes, and young dragonflies spend their lives in the pool. As we sit here, we wonder how many thousands of other little aquaria are all around us, hidden from our eyes!

Plants climb the trees in the tropics, and so do the animals. The kinkajou over there is a soft little bundle of fur with large eyes. It has a special kind of tail that can be used as an extra hand. This helps it to hang down from the branches and reach the fruit it loves to eat. It is quiet now, but it will play and eat tonight. It is a relative of the raccoon, but unlike its northern cousin, the kinkajou has left the ground and spends its whole life in the trees.

A relative of the giant anteater also walks among the branches up here. The tamandua, or lesser anteater, is about half the size of its ground-floor relative. It has a grasping tail that fits it for living in the trees. It feasts on ants and termites. There are plenty of ant and termite nests in the trees for the anteater to tear open with its sharp claws. The ants live in every nook and cranny. Some of them nest in leaves; others build papery hanging nests on the branches. The termite nests are of all shapes and sizes, too. Some look like black footballs, some like mudcakes, and others like lumps of clay plastered on the branches. Over fifty thousand ants and termites were found in one tamandua's stomach.

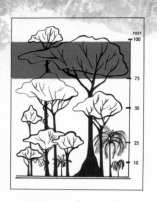

Now for the most wonderful place in the jungle. We are going to explore the upper forest canopy—seventy to a hundred feet from the ground. We sit on a seat fastened to a rope that runs through a pulley high in the trees. Up, up we go through the deep green low jungle and the flowery middle jungle to a new place. Here sunshine sparkles on the leaves, and the animal tenants are monkeys!

What a great time they seem to be having on the swinging vines and swaying branches! Watch the spider monkeys—the trapeze artists of the jungle! They hang by their long tails and take flying leaps through the air with their long, skinny arms and legs outstretched.

A sudden crashing in a nearby tree makes us turn. A clan of capuchin or white-faced monkeys is shaking leaves at us. We know their little faces well, for monkeys like these hop about with the organ-grinders on city streets and pick out fortunes for us. But this is their real home. Look at the bunch of them skip and jump and run and hurl themselves through space to another branch. They can hold on with their tails, too.

The capuchin and spider monkeys use their tails like a fifth hand. So do a lot of other monkeys here in the American tropical jungles. But what about monkeys in other parts of the world? You would expect them to have such handy tails, too. And yet they do not. The monkeys of Asia and Africa cannot use their tails this way. They are not as "specialized" for tree living as the monkeys of America.

But even here some of the monkeys do not have grasping tails. Those saki monkeys who are making faces at us cannot hold on with their tails. We can't help laughing at them. They look like little old men with black beards and black hair neatly parted in the middle. They move slowly away through the forest canopy, turning to stare at us every once in a while.

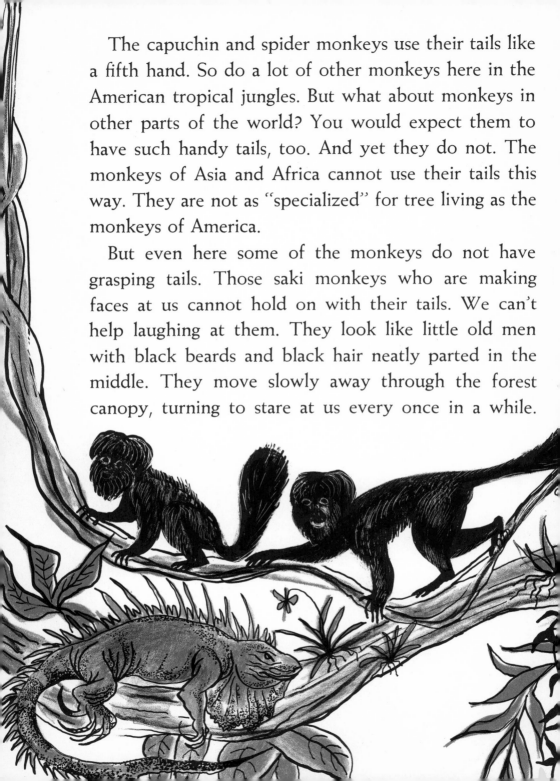

Watching the monkeys was so much fun that we almost missed the strangest-looking lizard we have ever seen—the iguana lizard, with a row of spines along its back and a flap of skin under its chin. It really looks like something left over from the age of dinosaurs, when bigger and fiercer-looking relatives of this lizard walked the earth.

Another of these leftovers is the sloth, hanging upside down near the iguana lizard. For most of its life it lives in a topsy-turvy world, moving upside down, eating upside down, and sleeping upside down. It doesn't do much except pick leaves from the trees to eat. Maybe this animal lasted through the ages in these forests because it is so hard to see as it hangs from the branches. Tiny microscopic green plants called algae grow in its hair and make it look like the shaggy moss hanging on the tree.

And now our swinging chair goes up to the roof of the rain forest. Now we are above the millions of leaves that sheltered us. The hot sun of the tropics beats down on our heads. The wind blows around us. Our feet dangle over the treetops. Below us they look like a carpet of green sprinkled with flowers. The trees and vines have grown up and up through the dim layers of the forest until they reached the sunlight here and burst into flower. Some of the trees and vines bear clusters of red and yellow and brown fruit. Here at the top of the rain forest we find the same blaze of color we saw in the jungle clearing. Over that tree covered with yellow blossoms clouds of golden butterflies are hovering.

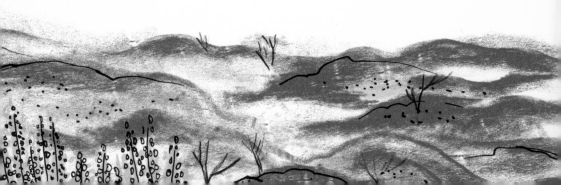

A crowd of brilliant birds has gathered to pick the ripe fruit. We have seen the parrots and their larger cousins, the macaws, at the zoo. Both have sharply hooked bills with which they easily crack open nuts and seeds. Look carefully at their feet. They have four toes, two pointing backward and two forward—a good toe arrangement for grasping branches and climbing.

The toucans are the queerest-looking birds in the group. Their huge beaks are one third as long as their bodies. They look like clowns with masks.

There are hummingbirds here, too. They gather wherever there is nectar to suck from flowers. Right now they are buzzing around the blossoms on a wallaba tree.

Suddenly we hear a terrible noise, halfway between a roar and a howl. It is so loud that we tremble and hang on for dear life to the ropes of our chair. What can be making such a frightful sound up here at the top of the jungle?

Then we notice that in the giant tree sticking up above the rest there are nearly a dozen howler monkeys. Some of them have babies hanging on to them, but this doesn't seem to interfere with their jumping around in the trees. Watch their tails hold on to the branches. These monkeys are bigger than any of the others we have seen. Now they are quiet again, and we are certainly glad.

MONKEY'S TAIL

UNDERSIDE OF GECKO'S TOES

IGUANA'S CLAWS

PARROT'S CLAWS

From bottom to top the tropical rain forest is packed with animals and plants. We see different kinds of plants and animals as we climb up through the forest because the forest climate changes from the ground to the treetops. The air is damp and cool on the forest floor and gets drier and warmer as we go up. The light is dimmest at the bottom and gets gradually brighter toward the top. Each layer of the forest, with its own climate, has its own special plant and animal tenants. The same thing is true of every forest in the world. But in the rain forest, where there are so many more tree layers, much more animal and plant life has moved into the trees.

No wonder the animals and plants of the tropical American rain forest are suited to tree life in so many ways. This is the home of the tail that can grasp a branch and hold on. Most of the monkeys, the kinkajou, and the anteaters that live in the trees have such tails. Many of the forest lizards have sticky pads on their toes that help them to hold on to the branches. The iguana lizard has strong toenails. Parrots and macaws have toes particularly suited to climbing.

LIANA

TENDRILS

PHILODENDRON

The plants of the rain forest get up into the trees, too. There are more kinds of climbing plants here than any other place on earth. Some, like Philodendron, climb by sending out little roots along the way. Others make circles in the air as they grow and twine around any support near them. Still others grow little threads called tendrils that can attach themselves to bark or stems or leaves.

The air plants have their own special way of living in the trees. They use the trees as perches and catch water and bits of soil in their roots or in their clasping leaves.

AIR PLANTS

The rain forest of South America is very, very old. It has been there for over a hundred million years. When the forests in other parts of the world were destroyed by long periods of very cold or very dry weather, the jungle remained. Perhaps that is why it is like a museum where we can see living plants and animals like those that once lived in other parts of the world. We know that there were tapirs over much of North America, Europe, and Asia twenty million years ago. Today they are gone—except in the jungles around the Equator. Armadillos, anteaters, and sloths are other odd-looking leftovers of bygone days. Once they lived in many other parts of the world, but today they are found mostly in the tropical rain forest. If we want to see a live tree fern, we have to go to the tropics. They have disappeared everywhere else.

TAPIR

SOME LEFTOVERS
OF BYGONE DAYS

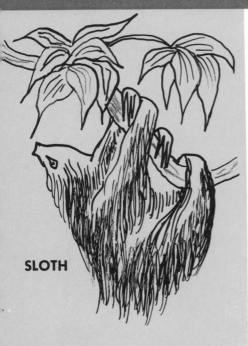
SLOTH

TREE FERN

ARMADILLO

GREAT ANTEATER

We have seen through the rain forest from bottom to top. We have seen animals and plants that live and grow in many ways that are new to us. But they are not really "strange," for they are well suited to the jungle home where they live.